Pescatarian Meal Ideas

40+ Curated and Healthy Low-Carb Pescatarian Recipes for Lunch and Dinner (Includes Instant Pot Recipes)

mf

copyright © 2020 Bruce Ackerberg

All rights reserved No part of this book may be reproduced, or stored in a retrieval system, or transmitted in any form or by any means, electronic, mechanical, photocopying, recording, or otherwise, without express written permission of the publisher.

Disclaimer

By reading this disclaimer, you are accepting the terms of the disclaimer in full. If you disagree with this disclaimer, please do not read the guide.

All of the content within this guide is provided for informational and educational purposes only, and should not be accepted as independent medical or other professional advice. The author is not a doctor, physician, nurse, mental health provider, or registered nutritionist/dietician. Therefore, using and reading this guide does not establish any form of a physician-patient relationship.

Always consult with a physician or another qualified health provider with any issues or questions you might have regarding any sort of medical condition. Do not ever disregard any qualified professional medical advice or delay seeking that advice because of anything you have read in this guide. The information in this guide is not intended to be any sort of medical advice and should not be used in lieu of any medical advice by a licensed and qualified medical professional.

The information in this guide has been compiled from a variety of known sources. However, the author cannot attest to or guarantee the accuracy of each source and thus should not be held liable for any errors or omissions.

You acknowledge that the publisher of this guide will not be held liable for any loss or damage of any kind incurred as a result of this guide or the reliance on any information provided within this guide. You acknowledge and agree that you assume all risk and responsibility for any action you undertake in response to the information in this guide.

Using this guide does not guarantee any particular result (e.g., weight loss or a cure). By reading this guide, you acknowledge that there are no guarantees to any specific outcome or results you can expect.

All product names, diet plans, or names used in this guide are for identification purposes only and are the property of their respective owners. The use of these names does not imply endorsement. All other trademarks cited herein are the property of their respective owners.

Where applicable, this guide is not intended to be a substitute for the original work of this diet plan and is, at most, a supplement to the original work for this diet plan and never a direct substitute. This guide is a personal expression of the facts of that diet plan.

Where applicable, persons shown in the cover images are stock photography models and the publisher has obtained the rights to use the images through license agreements with third-party stock image companies.

Table of Contents

Introduction	8
Becoming Pescatarian	10
Enter the Pescatarian Diet	10
Tips for Successfully Adopting a Pescatarian Diet	12
Why Should You Adopt the Pescatarian Diet?	15
Potential Drawbacks of the Diet	17
Foods to Eat	19
Vegetables	19
Fruits	19
Whole Grains	19
Legumes	20
Nuts and Seeds	20
Fish and Seafood	20
Dairy and Eggs (if included)	20
Healthy Fats	21
Herbs and Spices	21
Beverages	21
Foods to Avoid	22
Meat and Poultry	22
Processed Meats	22
Animal By-products (if following a stricter pescatarian diet)	22
Processed Foods	23
Unhealthy Fats	23
Dairy Products (if following a dairy-free variant)	23
Eggs (if following an egg-free variant)	23
Certain Condiments and Additives	24
Alcohol (in excess)	24
Recipes	25
Arugula with Roasted Garlic Fig Dressing	26

Lemon-Herb Grilled Shrimp Skewers	28
Beets with Onions, Balsamic Vinegar, and Rosemary	30
Broccoli Salad	32
Carrot and Cashew Soup	34
Cucumber with Fennel and Creamy Avocado Dressing	36
Haddock Tacos	37
Seafood Stew	39
Shrimp Taco Salad	41
Trout Scrambler	43
Cornmeal Catfish	45
Tomato Clams	47
Cod Burger	49
Cod Pea Curry	51
Baked Flounder	53
Sweet Potatoes and Mackerel	54
Salmon Salad	56
Seared Salmon	58
Tahini Salmon	60
Broiled Sardines	62
Grilled Shrimp	63
Tilapia Sticks	65
Summer-Time Trout	67
Lemon Trout	69
Instant Pot Recipes	**70**
Fish Fillet Instant Pot	71
Brazilian-Style Fish Stew	73
Fish Curry (Indian Style)	75
Spinach and Rice Haddock	77
Fish Steak Surprise	79
Tomato Basil and Tilapia	81
Spanish Rice	83

Instant Pot Broccoli	85
Instant Pot Cauliflower	86
Split Pea Soup	87
Tacos and Lentils	89
Vegetable Soup	91
Fast Instant Pot Salmon (For Frozen Ones)	93
Hummus for Instapot	95
Salmon and Vegetables	97
Shrimp Paella	99
Tomato Basil Soup	102
Kale Soup with Sweet Potatoes and Lentils	104
Instant Pot Lemon Pepper Salmon	106
Cheesy Lentils with Brown Rice	108
Conclusion	**110**
Frequently Asked Questions for New Pescatarians	**114**
References and Helpful Links	**117**

Introduction

Are you aware that nearly one-third of Americans are living with chronic health issues? Over the latter part of the 20th century, the American diet drastically shifted, leading many to favor fast food. While we're all too familiar with the negative health impacts of fast food, resisting the allure of a triple patty burger can be incredibly challenging.

But what if there was a natural way to enhance your health and shed some extra pounds? Enter the Pescatarian Diet—a predominantly vegetarian diet accented with seafood. Unlike traditional vegetarianism, this diet incorporates the nutritional benefits of seafood along with wholesome vegetables. Widely embraced in Mediterranean regions, the Pescatarian Diet is renowned for contributing to the impressive longevity of its followers.

This cookbook is your gateway to the vibrant world of Pescatarian cuisine, offering a carefully selected array of mouthwatering recipes designed to delight your palate and nourish your body.

In this guide, you'll uncover:

- Key Benefits of Pescetarianism
- 40 Delicious Pescatarian Recipes (including Instant Pot and other cooking methods)

Keep reading to discover how the Pescatarian Diet can transform your health and elevate your culinary experiences.

Becoming Pescatarian

For as long as we have studied the foods we consume, there has been an ongoing quest to discover the optimal diet. With the media spotlight on the prevalence of chronic diseases such as heart disease, diabetes, and obesity, the urgency to find the right diet has never been greater. This demand has given rise to numerous diets, many of which are plagued by a fatal flaw—they are simply impractical for long-term adherence.

The inherent difficulties of these various diets often lead individuals astray, setting them up for failure. Many people struggle to maintain a diet because it is designed in a way that makes success nearly impossible.

Enter the Pescatarian Diet

If you're reading this, you might already have a basic understanding of what a Pescatarian diet entails. Essentially, it is a vegetarian diet where the primary sources of protein come from seafood and fish instead of meat and poultry.

The Pescatarian Diet is often hailed as the perfect balance, combining the delicious flavors and nutritional benefits of a seafood diet with the health advantages of a vegetarian lifestyle.

This diet is particularly popular in Mediterranean regions, where people consume plenty of vegetables and fish—a combination that contributes to their impressive longevity, with many living well beyond 100 years. The term "Pescatarian" emerged in the early 1990s, derived from the Italian word "Pesce," meaning fish, and "vegetarian." It's also known as the Pesco-Vegetarian Diet.

Technically a subset of vegetarianism, the Pescatarian Diet primarily consists of plant-based foods, with seafood serving as a vital source of protein.

While there are other protein sources within a vegetarian diet, the Pescatarian approach not only provides sufficient protein but also enhances nutritional intake. The inclusion of seafood offers additional benefits, such as heart-healthy omega-3 fatty acids.

Despite the numerous advantages of the Pescatarian Diet, some individuals may remain skeptical about its effectiveness and whether it will truly work for them.

Tips for Successfully Adopting a Pescatarian Diet

Now that we have addressed some common questions about the Pescatarian diet, here are a few tips to help you successfully adopt this lifestyle:

1. **Recognizing the Challenges**

    Research from UCLA reveals that two-thirds of people who attempt diets fail. Even more concerning, those who fail often regain a substantial amount of weight. With every new diet, the odds seem stacked against you. However, statistics don't have to dictate your outcome. Here are some essential tips to help you succeed and achieve your health goals.

2. **Changing Your Mindset**

    For many, dieting means enduring meals they dislike. Viewing diets as necessary evils sets you up for failure. People naturally resist change, especially when it's unpleasant. Society values food for taste and convenience, contributing to fast food culture. Switching from burgers and pizza to new tastes can be jarring and unpleasant, eventually leading to dietary failure as enthusiasm wanes.

3. **Gradual Integration**

   Medical literature suggests that gradual changes are more likely to yield success than drastic ones. For instance, individuals who gradually quit smoking are more successful than those who go cold turkey. Similarly, incorporating dietary changes slowly allows your body to adjust, increasing the likelihood of adherence. Start by integrating aspects of the new diet into your life little by little until it becomes fully incorporated.

4. **Establishing Habits**

   Introducing any new practice gradually—whether a hobby or a dietary change—makes it harder to reject. Abrupt changes feel external and unnatural, leading to easy rejection. Ingraining the new diet as a habit makes it a natural part of daily life, making it more resistant to displacement. Developing a habit around your newfound diet is already half the battle.

5. **Enjoying the Process**

   Many diets feel like autocratic regimes, dictating strict adherence. While it's important to follow dietary guidelines, it doesn't mean you should toil over every detail. Enjoying your diet is crucial for long-term success. Enthusiasm might get you started, but genuine enjoyment will keep you going.

6. **Experimentation and Customization**

    To make your diet more enjoyable, experiment with different dishes within your food groups. Mix and match foods to your liking and seek out recipes from others who have customized meals to suit their tastes. Making each dish your own transforms every meal into both an achievement and an enjoyable experience.

By understanding these tips and integrating them into your approach, you can increase your chances of successfully adopting the pescatarian diet. For more detailed guidance, refer to the following chapters in this book. Welcome to the pescatarian lifestyle, and happy eating!

Why Should You Adopt the Pescatarian Diet?

The Pescatarian diet is certainly no magic bullet but it has proven its ability to help people in a wide array of matters and health issues. Proof of this diet's ability to improve health is in the numbers. Looking at the population of people living in the Mediterranean, they have enjoyed lives existing in the three-digit space—more than what normal Americans could ask for.

If numbers are not enough to highlight the ability of this diet, here are some of the benefits you might enjoy with a Pescatarian diet.

1. **Weight Loss**

    The primary purpose of a weight loss regimen is to eat fewer calories than our body uses up. If you reverse the process, we get fat as a by-product of our body storing the extra calories. The Pescatarian diet's focus on fibers will make many feel fuller for longer which will prevent the unneeded intake of high caloric foods.

2. **A Habit Maker**

   As mentioned, a lot, the way the diet is designed is that it is enjoyable. The diet does not force you into eating expensive and rare foods for it to work. The traits of the diet make it enjoyable to do and the more that we enjoy something the easier it is to integrate into our routines – forming a habit!

3. **Fun and Enjoyable**

   Fish and other seafood are a very delectable choice of food groups. Such food groups are the nearest anybody could get while still reaping the benefits of healthy living while still looking forward to the taste of each meal.

4. **Slowing Down Your Metabolism**

   When people go into diets and lessen their calorie intake compared to their calorie use, the body slows down their metabolism. With a lesser amount of calories being used, weight loss can look like an uphill battle. However, the Pescatarian diet has metabolism-boosting food groups that lessen such effects.

Even with the benefits listed here, the Pescatarian diet still has a lot more to supply us. Surely, as we accumulate more and more research about this diet, we will find more information about its benefits. While we wait, one thing can be certain about this diet – it is a definite boost to our health.

If you want to start following the Pescatarian diet, head on to the next chapter to see the recipes.

Potential Drawbacks of the Diet

While the pescatarian diet offers numerous benefits, it's important to consider some potential disadvantages. Understanding these challenges can help you make an informed decision about whether this diet is right for you.

1. **Limited Protein Sources**

   Although fish and seafood provide excellent protein, a pescatarian diet limits your options compared to diets that include poultry, beef, and pork. You might need to be more creative with your meals to ensure you're getting a variety of protein sources.

2. **Risk of Mercury Exposure**

   Certain types of fish, like tuna and swordfish, can contain high levels of mercury. Consuming these fish frequently can lead to mercury accumulation in your body, which poses health risks. It's crucial to choose fish wisely and opt for those with lower mercury levels, such as salmon, sardines, and trout.

3. **Dietary Imbalance**

   Relying heavily on seafood could potentially lead to an imbalance of nutrients if not carefully planned. For example, while fish provide omega-3 fatty acids, they might lack other essential nutrients like iron and vitamin B12, which are abundant in red meat. Supplementing or finding alternative sources of these nutrients is necessary.

4. **Cost Considerations**

   Seafood can be more expensive than other protein sources like chicken or beans. This might make a pescatarian diet less affordable for some individuals, particularly if you aim to buy fresh and sustainably sourced fish.

While there are some challenges associated with the pescatarian diet—such as limited protein sources, potential mercury exposure, and higher costs—the numerous health and environmental benefits make it a worthwhile consideration. With mindful planning and thoughtful choices, you can enjoy a balanced, nutritious, and sustainable diet that supports both your health and the planet.

Foods to Eat

A pescatarian diet primarily includes plant-based foods and fish or other seafood. Here are the main food categories and examples:

Vegetables

- Leafy greens: spinach, kale, arugula
- Cruciferous vegetables: broccoli, cauliflower, Brussels sprouts
- Root vegetables: carrots, beets, sweet potatoes
- Others: bell peppers, zucchini, asparagus

Fruits

- Berries: strawberries, blueberries, raspberries
- Citrus: oranges, lemons, grapefruits
- Tropical: mangoes, pineapples, bananas
- Others: apples, pears, grapes

Whole Grains

- Brown rice
- Quinoa

- Oats
- Barley
- Whole wheat products: bread, pasta

Legumes

- Lentils
- Chickpeas
- Black beans
- Peas

Nuts and Seeds

- Almonds
- Walnuts
- Chia seeds
- Flaxseeds
- Sunflower seeds

Fish and Seafood

- Fatty fish: salmon, mackerel, sardines
- Whitefish: cod, haddock, tilapia
- Shellfish: shrimp, crab, lobster
- Mollusks: clams, mussels, oysters

Dairy and Eggs (if included)

- Milk
- Cheese

- Yogurt
- Eggs

Healthy Fats

- Olive oil
- Avocado
- Coconut oil

Herbs and Spices

- Basil
- Cilantro
- Rosemary
- Turmeric
- Ginger

Beverages

- Water
- Herbal teas
- Coffee (in moderation)

These foods provide a balanced diet rich in nutrients, ensuring you get a good mix of protein, healthy fats, vitamins, and minerals.

Foods to Avoid

In a pescatarian diet, the primary foods to avoid are those that come from land animals, along with certain processed and unhealthy options. Here is a list of foods to avoid:

Meat and Poultry

- Beef
- Pork
- Chicken
- Turkey
- Lamb

Processed Meats

- Bacon
- Sausages
- Ham
- Deli meats

Animal By-products (if following a stricter pescatarian diet)

- Gelatin (unless it's sourced from fish)

- Some animal-based broths and stocks

Processed Foods
- Fast food items
- Packaged snacks high in sodium and trans fats
- Sugary desserts and candies

Unhealthy Fats
- Trans fats (found in some margarines and packaged baked goods)
- High amounts of saturated fats (often found in fried foods)

Dairy Products (if following a dairy-free variant)
- Milk
- Cheese
- Butter
- Cream

Eggs (if following an egg-free variant)
- Any form of eggs including boiled, scrambled, or baked into products

Certain Condiments and Additives

- Sauces and dressings containing animal fats or meat extracts
- Some Worcestershire sauces (which may contain anchovies, though these are technically okay but usually avoided by strict vegetarians)
- Meat-based seasoning mixes

Alcohol (in excess)

- Beer, wine, and spirits should be consumed in moderation as part of a healthy lifestyle

By avoiding these foods, you can adhere to the principles of a pescatarian diet, which emphasizes plant-based foods and seafood for health and ethical reasons.

Recipes

Arugula with Roasted Garlic Fig Dressing

Ingredients:

For the Salad:

- 4 cups fresh arugula
- 1/2 cup cherry tomatoes, halved
- 1/4 cup red onion, thinly sliced
- 1/4 cup feta cheese, crumbled (optional)
- 1/4 cup walnuts, toasted
- Salt and pepper to taste

For the Roasted Garlic Fig Dressing:

- 4 cloves garlic, unpeeled
- 1/4 cup dried figs, chopped
- 3 tablespoons balsamic vinegar
- 1 tablespoon honey or maple syrup
- 1/3 cup extra-virgin olive oil
- Salt and pepper to taste

Instructions:

1. Preheat your oven to 400°F (200°C).
2. Place the garlic cloves on a baking sheet and roast for 15-20 minutes, until they are soft and golden brown.
3. In a small bowl, combine the roasted garlic cloves, chopped figs, balsamic vinegar, honey or maple syrup, and olive oil. Use an immersion blender or traditional blender to blend until smooth.

4. Season with salt and pepper to taste.
5. In a large salad bowl, add the arugula, cherry tomatoes, red onion, feta cheese (if using), and walnuts, and toss with the roasted garlic fig dressing.
6. Serve and enjoy!

Lemon-Herb Grilled Shrimp Skewers

Ingredients:

- 1 pound large shrimp, peeled and deveined
- 2 tablespoons olive oil
- 2 tablespoons lemon juice
- 2 cloves garlic, minced
- 1 tablespoon fresh parsley, chopped
- 1 tablespoon fresh dill, chopped
- 1 tablespoon fresh basil, chopped
- Salt and pepper to taste
- Lemon wedges, for serving

Instructions:

1. In a small bowl, whisk together the olive oil, lemon juice, minced garlic, chopped parsley, dill, and basil.
2. Season the shrimp with salt and pepper on both sides.
3. Pour the marinade over the shrimp and toss until well-coated.
4. Cover and refrigerate for 30 minutes to an hour.
5. Preheat your grill to medium-high heat.

6. Thread the marinated shrimp on skewers (if using wooden skewers, soak them in water for at least 20 minutes beforehand to prevent burning).
7. Grill the shrimp for 2-3 minutes on each side, until they are pink and opaque.
8. Serve the grilled shrimp skewers with lemon wedges on the side for squeezing over top.

Beets with Onions, Balsamic Vinegar, and Rosemary

Ingredients:

- 4 medium beets, scrubbed and trimmed
- 1 large red onion, thinly sliced
- 2 tablespoons olive oil
- 3 tablespoons balsamic vinegar
- 1 tablespoon fresh rosemary, chopped (or 1 teaspoon dried rosemary)
- Salt and pepper to taste
- Fresh parsley, for garnish (optional)

Instructions:

1. Preheat your oven to 400 degrees F (200 degrees C).
2. Wrap each beet individually in foil and place them on a baking sheet.
3. Roast the beets for 45 minutes to an hour, or until they are tender when pierced with a fork.
4. Let the beets cool, then peel off the skin and slice into wedges.
5. In a large skillet, heat the olive oil over medium heat.
6. Add the sliced onions and cook until they are soft and translucent, about 8-10 minutes.
7. Stir in the balsamic vinegar and chopped rosemary, and cook for an additional 2-3 minutes.

8. Add the roasted beet wedges to the skillet and toss until they are coated in the balsamic mixture.
9. Cook for another 1-2 minutes, until the beets are heated through.
10. Season with salt and pepper to taste.
11. Serve the beets with onions, balsamic vinegar, and rosemary hot or at room temperature.
12. Garnish with fresh parsley, if desired.

Broccoli Salad

Ingredients:

- 4 cups fresh broccoli florets
- 1/2 cup red onion, finely chopped
- 1/2 cup dried cranberries
- 1/2 cup sunflower seeds
- 8 slices of bacon, cooked until crispy and crumbled
- 1 cup shredded cheddar cheese

Dressing:

- 1 cup mayonnaise
- 2 tablespoons white wine vinegar
- 1/4 cup granulated sugar
- Salt and pepper to taste

Instructions:

1. In a large mixing bowl, combine the broccoli florets, red onion, dried cranberries, sunflower seeds, crumbled bacon, and shredded cheddar cheese.
2. In a separate small mixing bowl, whisk together the mayonnaise, vinegar, sugar, salt, and pepper until well combined.
3. Pour the dressing over the broccoli mixture and toss to coat evenly.
4. Cover and refrigerate for at least 30 minutes before serving to allow flavors to meld together.

5. Serve cold as a side dish or add protein such as grilled chicken or tofu for a complete meal.
6. Leftovers can be stored in an airtight container in the refrigerator for up to 2-3 days.

Enjoy this tasty and nutritious broccoli salad as a refreshing addition to any meal or as a light lunch option.

Carrot and Cashew Soup

Ingredients:

- 1 lb carrots, peeled and chopped
- 1 cup raw cashews
- 1 medium onion, chopped
- 2 cloves garlic, minced
- 1 inch fresh ginger, grated
- 4 cups vegetable broth
- 1 cup coconut milk
- 2 tablespoons olive oil
- Salt and pepper to taste
- Fresh cilantro for garnish (optional)

Instructions:

1. In a large pot, heat the olive oil over medium heat. Add in the chopped onion and cook until translucent, about 5 minutes.
2. Add in the minced garlic and grated ginger and cook for an additional 1-2 minutes.
3. Stir in the chopped carrots and cashews, coating them with the mixture in the pot.
4. Pour in the vegetable broth and bring to a boil. Reduce heat to low and let simmer for 20-25 minutes, or until carrots are tender.
5. Once carrots are cooked through, remove from heat and let cool slightly before transferring the mixture to

a blender or using an immersion blender to blend until smooth.
6. Return the blended mixture to the pot and stir in the coconut milk. Season with salt and pepper to taste.
7. Serve hot, garnished with fresh cilantro if desired.

Cucumber with Fennel and Creamy Avocado Dressing

Ingredients:

- 2 large cucumbers, sliced
- 1 fennel bulb, thinly sliced
- 1 ripe avocado
- ½ cup plain Greek yogurt
- 2 tablespoons fresh lemon juice
- 1 tablespoon olive oil
- 1 clove garlic, minced
- Salt and pepper to taste
- Fresh dill for garnish (optional)

Instructions:

1. In a small mixing bowl, mash the ripe avocado until smooth.
2. Stir in the Greek yogurt, lemon juice, olive oil, and minced garlic until well combined.
3. Season with salt and pepper to taste.
4. In a large bowl, mix together the sliced cucumbers and fennel.
5. Pour the creamy avocado dressing over the vegetables and toss until evenly coated.
6. Serve chilled, garnished with fresh dill if desired.

Haddock Tacos

Ingredients:

- 1 lb haddock filets
- 1 tablespoon olive oil
- 1 teaspoon cumin
- 1 teaspoon paprika
- 1 teaspoon garlic powder
- ½ teaspoon chili powder
- Salt and pepper to taste
- 8 small corn tortillas
- 1 cup shredded cabbage
- ½ cup diced tomatoes
- ¼ cup chopped red onion
- ¼ cup chopped fresh cilantro
- 1 lime, cut into wedges
- Hot sauce, for serving (optional)

Instructions:

1. Preheat the oven to 375°F.
2. Place the haddock filets on a baking sheet and drizzle with olive oil.
3. In a small bowl, mix together the cumin, paprika, garlic powder, chili powder, salt and pepper.
4. Sprinkle the spice mixture over the haddock filets.
5. Bake for 12-15 minutes or until the fish flakes easily with a fork.

6. While the haddock is cooking, warm up the tortillas in a pan over medium heat for about 20 seconds per side.
7. Assemble tacos by placing a few pieces of cooked haddock in each tortilla and topping with shredded cabbage, diced tomatoes, red onion, and cilantro.
8. Squeeze fresh lime juice over the tacos and serve with hot sauce if desired. Enjoy your tasty and healthy Haddock Tacos!

Seafood Stew

Ingredients:

- 1 pound haddock filets
- 2 tablespoons olive oil
- 1 teaspoon ground cumin
- 1 teaspoon paprika
- 1 teaspoon garlic powder
- ½ teaspoon chili powder
- Salt and pepper to taste
- 8 small corn tortillas
- 1 cup shredded cabbage
- ½ cup diced tomatoes
- ¼ cup chopped red onion
- ¼ cup chopped fresh cilantro
- 1 lime, cut into wedges
- Hot sauce, for serving (optional)

Instructions:

1. In a large pot or Dutch oven, heat 2 tablespoons of olive oil over medium heat.
2. Season the haddock filets with cumin, paprika, garlic powder, chili powder, salt and pepper.
3. Add the seasoned fish to the pot and cook for about 5 minutes on each side until lightly browned.
4. Remove the fish from the pot and set aside.

5. In the same pot, add diced onion and cook until translucent.
6. Stir in minced garlic and cook for an additional minute.
7. Pour in 4 cups of chicken broth (or vegetable broth) and bring to a simmer.
8. Add in chopped potatoes, carrots, celery, and any other desired vegetables.
9. Simmer for 15-20 minutes or until the vegetables are tender.
10. Flake the cooked haddock into bite-sized pieces and add back into the pot.
11. Season with salt and pepper to taste.
12. Serve hot in bowls with crusty bread on the side for dipping.
13. Garnish with fresh parsley or cilantro if desired. Enjoy your delicious Seafood Stew!

Shrimp Taco Salad

Ingredients:

- 1 lb raw shrimp, peeled and deveined
- 2 tbsp olive oil
- 1 tsp chili powder
- 1 tsp cumin
- 1/2 tsp paprika
- 1/4 tsp garlic powder
- 1/4 tsp onion powder
- Salt and pepper to taste
- 4 cups chopped romaine lettuce
- 1 cup black beans, drained and rinsed
- 1 cup corn kernels (fresh or frozen)
- 1 cup halved cherry tomatoes
- 1/2 cup diced red onion
- 1 avocado, diced
- 1/4 cup chopped fresh cilantro
- 1 lime, cut into wedges
- Tortilla strips for garnish (optional)
- Your favorite salad dressing or salsa

Instructions:

1. In a small bowl, mix together the chili powder, cumin, paprika, garlic powder, onion powder, salt and pepper.
2. Heat olive oil in a large skillet over medium-high heat.

3. Add the shrimp to the skillet and sprinkle with the spice mixture.
4. Cook for 2-3 minutes on each side or until shrimp is pink and opaque.
5. Remove from heat and set aside.
6. In a large serving bowl, combine lettuce, black beans, corn kernels, cherry tomatoes, red onion, and avocado.
7. Top with cooked shrimp and sprinkle with chopped cilantro.
8. Squeeze lime wedges over the salad.
9. Optional: Add tortilla strips for extra crunch and texture.
10. Serve with your favorite dressing or salsa on the side. Enjoy your flavorful Shrimp Taco Salad!

Trout Scrambler

Ingredients:

- 8 ounces smoked trout, flaked
- 6 large eggs
- 1/4 cup whole milk or cream
- 1 tablespoon butter
- 1/4 cup diced bell pepper (any color)
- 1/4 cup diced red onion
- 1 tablespoon chopped fresh chives
- Salt and pepper to taste
- Fresh parsley for garnish (optional)
- Toast or warm tortillas, for serving

Instructions:

1. In a medium bowl, beat the eggs and milk or cream together until well combined.
2. Heat butter in a large skillet over medium heat.
3. Add diced bell pepper and red onion to the skillet and cook for 2-3 minutes or until softened.
4. Pour the egg mixture into the skillet and stir gently with a spatula, allowing the eggs to cook evenly.
5. Once the eggs are about halfway cooked, add the flaked smoked trout to the skillet and continue stirring gently.
6. Cook until eggs are fully set and fluffy, about 4-5 minutes.

7. Sprinkle chopped chives and season with salt and pepper to taste.
8. Serve the Trout Scrambler hot, garnished with fresh parsley if desired.
9. Enjoy for breakfast or brunch, served on toast or wrapped in warm tortillas for a tasty twist.

Cornmeal Catfish

Ingredients:

- 4 catfish filets
- 1 cup cornmeal
- 1/2 cup all-purpose flour
- 1 teaspoon salt
- 1/2 teaspoon black pepper
- 1/2 teaspoon garlic powder
- 1/2 teaspoon paprika
- 1/4 teaspoon cayenne pepper (optional)
- 1 cup buttermilk
- Vegetable oil for frying
- Lemon wedges for serving
- Fresh parsley for garnish (optional)

Instructions:

1. In a shallow dish, mix together the cornmeal, flour, salt, black pepper, garlic powder, paprika, and cayenne pepper (if desired).
2. In another shallow dish, pour the buttermilk.
3. Dip each catfish filet in the buttermilk and then coat evenly with the cornmeal mixture.
4. Heat vegetable oil in a large skillet over medium heat until hot.

5. Place the coated catfish filets in the skillet and fry for about 4-5 minutes on each side or until golden brown and crispy.
6. Remove from heat and place on a paper towel-lined plate to absorb excess oil.
7. Serve the Cornmeal Catfish hot, garnished with lemon wedges and fresh parsley if desired.
8. Pair with your favorite sides, such as coleslaw or mac and cheese for a delicious Southern-inspired meal.

Tomato Clams

Ingredients:

- 2 pounds fresh clams, scrubbed and debearded
- 2 tablespoons olive oil
- 4 cloves garlic, minced
- 1 shallot, finely chopped
- 1/2 cup dry white wine
- 1 (14.5-ounce) can of diced tomatoes, undrained
- 1/2 teaspoon red pepper flakes (optional)
- Salt and black pepper, to taste
- 1/4 cup fresh parsley, chopped
- 1 lemon, cut into wedges

Instructions:

1. In a large pot, heat olive oil over medium-high heat.
2. Add minced garlic and chopped shallot, sautéing for 1-2 minutes until fragrant.
3. Pour in dry white wine and let it simmer for another minute.
4. Add the can of diced tomatoes (with juice) to the pot, stirring to combine with the wine mixture.
5. If desired, sprinkle in red pepper flakes for added heat.
6. Allow tomato mixture to simmer for about 5 minutes, then add in cleaned clams.
7. Stir everything together gently and cover with a lid.

8. Let the clams cook for about 8-10 minutes, or until all shells have opened.
9. Discard any unopened shells and season with salt and black pepper to taste.
10. Serve hot in a large bowl, garnished with fresh parsley and lemon wedges for squeezing over the clams before eating.

Cod Burger

Ingredients:

- 1 lb fresh cod filets, skinless and boneless
- 1 cup panko breadcrumbs
- 1 large egg, beaten
- 2 tablespoons mayonnaise
- 1 tablespoon Dijon mustard
- 1 lemon, zested and juiced
- 2 tablespoons fresh parsley, finely chopped
- 2 green onions, finely chopped
- Salt and black pepper to taste
- Olive oil for frying

To serve:

- 4 burger buns
- Lettuce leaves
- Tomato slices
- Sliced red onion
- Additional mayonnaise or tartar sauce

Instructions:

1. Begin by preparing the cod filets - pat them dry with paper towels and cut them into small chunks.
2. In a medium bowl, mix together the beaten egg, mayonnaise, Dijon mustard, lemon zest and juice,

parsley, green onions, salt, and black pepper until well combined.
3. Place the panko breadcrumbs in a separate shallow dish.
4. Dip each piece of cod into the egg mixture, then roll it in the panko breadcrumbs to evenly coat all sides.
5. Heat olive oil in a large skillet over medium-high heat.
6. Place coated cod filets in the hot pan and cook for about 3-4 minutes on each side or until golden brown.
7. Remove cooked filets from the skillet and place onto a paper towel-lined plate to drain excess oil.
8. To assemble the burgers, lightly toast the burger buns in a separate pan or on a grill.
9. Spread additional mayonnaise or tartar sauce onto the bottom bun, then add lettuce leaves, tomato slices, and sliced red onion.
10. Place one cod filet on top of the vegetables, followed by the top bun.
11. Serve immediately with your favorite sides like french fries or coleslaw.

Cod Pea Curry

Ingredients:

- 1 lb cod filets, cut into bite-sized pieces
- 1 cup green peas (fresh or frozen)
- 1 large onion, finely chopped
- 3 cloves garlic, minced
- 1-inch piece of ginger, minced
- 2 tablespoons olive oil
- 1 tablespoon curry powder
- 1 teaspoon turmeric powder
- 1 teaspoon ground cumin
- 1 teaspoon ground coriander
- 1 can (14 oz) coconut milk
- 1 cup diced tomatoes (fresh or canned)
- 1 tablespoon tomato paste
- Salt and black pepper to taste
- Fresh cilantro, chopped (for garnish)
- Cooked rice or naan bread (for serving)

Instructions:

1. In a large skillet, heat olive oil over medium-high heat.
2. Add chopped onion and cook until translucent.
3. Stir in minced garlic and ginger and cook for another minute.

4. Add curry powder, turmeric, cumin, coriander, salt, and black pepper to the skillet and mix well with the onions.
5. Pour in coconut milk and diced tomatoes, then stir in tomato paste.
6. Bring the mixture to a simmer and let it cook for 5 minutes.
7. Gently add cod pieces into the skillet, making sure they are covered by the sauce.
8. Cook for another 5-7 minutes until the cod is fully cooked and flakes easily with a fork.
9. Add green peas into the skillet and cook for an additional 2-3 minutes until they are heated through.
10. Serve hot over rice or with naan bread, garnished with fresh cilantro.

Baked Flounder

Ingredients:

- 4 flounder filets
- 2 tablespoons olive oil
- 1 lemon (sliced)
- 2 cloves garlic (minced)
- 1 teaspoon paprika
- 1 teaspoon dried thyme
- Salt and black pepper to taste
- Fresh parsley (chopped, for garnish)

Instructions:

1. Preheat your oven to 375°F (190°C).
2. In a small bowl, mix together olive oil, minced garlic, paprika, dried thyme, and salt and black pepper.
3. Place the flounder filets on a baking dish lined with parchment paper.
4. Brush the filets with the prepared olive oil mixture on both sides.
5. Place lemon slices on top of each filet.
6. Bake for 12-15 minutes until the fish is fully cooked and flakes easily with a fork.
7. Garnish with fresh parsley before serving hot.

Sweet Potatoes and Mackerel

Ingredients:

- 4 mackerel filets
- 2 large sweet potatoes (peeled and cubed)
- 2 tablespoons olive oil
- 1 teaspoon smoked paprika
- 1 teaspoon cumin seeds
- 1 red onion (thinly sliced)
- 1 red bell pepper (sliced)
- 2 cloves garlic (minced)
- Juice of 1 lemon
- Salt and black pepper to taste
- Fresh cilantro (chopped, for garnish)

Instructions:

1. Preheat your oven to 400°F (200°C).
2. In a small bowl, mix together olive oil, smoked paprika, cumin seeds, minced garlic, lemon juice, and salt and black pepper.
3. Place the sweet potato cubes on a baking sheet lined with parchment paper.
4. Drizzle the prepared olive oil mixture over the sweet potatoes and toss to coat evenly.
5. Bake for 20 minutes until the sweet potatoes are fork-tender.

6. Meanwhile, season the mackerel filets with salt and black pepper on both sides.
7. In a skillet over medium heat, cook the filets for 2-3 minutes on each side until fully cooked.
8. In the same skillet, add sliced red onion and bell pepper and cook for 2-3 minutes until softened.
9. Serve the mackerel filets over a bed of roasted sweet potatoes.
10. Garnish with chopped cilantro before serving hot.

Salmon Salad

Ingredients:

- 2 cups mixed greens (such as spinach, arugula, and lettuce)
- 1 cup cherry tomatoes, halved
- 1 cucumber, sliced
- 1 avocado, diced
- 1/4 red onion, thinly sliced
- 2 tablespoons capers
- 2 salmon filets
- 1 tablespoon olive oil
- Salt and black pepper to taste
- 1 lemon, sliced
- Fresh dill for garnish

For the Dressing:

- 1/4 cup extra-virgin olive oil
- 2 tablespoons lemon juice
- 1 teaspoon Dijon mustard
- 1 teaspoon honey
- Salt and black pepper to taste

Instructions:

1. Preheat your oven to 375°F (190°C).
2. Place the salmon filets on a baking sheet lined with parchment paper.

3. Drizzle olive oil over the salmon and season with salt and black pepper.
4. Top each filet with slices of lemon and a sprinkle of fresh dill.
5. Bake for 12-15 minutes until the salmon is fully cooked.
6. In a small bowl, whisk together extra-virgin olive oil, lemon juice, Dijon mustard, honey, salt and black pepper to make the dressing.
7. In a large mixing bowl, combine mixed greens, cherry tomatoes, cucumber, avocado, red onion, and capers.
8. Pour the dressing over the salad and toss to combine.
9. Divide the salad into two serving bowls.
10. Place a salmon filet on top of each salad bowl and serve immediately.
11. Garnish with fresh dill before serving for an extra burst of flavor.

Seared Salmon

Ingredients:

- 4 salmon filets (about 6 ounces each)
- Salt and black pepper to taste
- 2 tablespoons olive oil
- 1 lemon, thinly sliced
- 2 cloves garlic, minced
- 2 tablespoons unsalted butter
- Fresh dill for garnish

Instructions:

1. Season the salmon filets with salt and black pepper on both sides.
2. In a large skillet, heat olive oil over medium-high heat.
3. Place the salmon filets in the skillet and cook for 4-5 minutes on each side until golden brown and cooked through.
4. Remove the salmon from the skillet and set aside on a plate.
5. In the same skillet, add lemon slices and minced garlic. Cook for 1-2 minutes until fragrant.
6. Add butter to the skillet and stir until melted.
7. Spoon the lemon butter sauce over the salmon filets.

8. Garnish with fresh dill before serving for an extra burst of flavor.
9. Serve the seared salmon hot with your choice of sides or on top of a salad.

Enjoy this delicious and healthy meal packed with omega-3 fatty acids, protein, and nutrients from fresh ingredients.

Tahini Salmon

Ingredients:

- 4 salmon filets (about 6 ounces each)
- Salt and black pepper to taste
- 2 tablespoons olive oil
- 1 lemon, thinly sliced
- 2 cloves garlic, minced
- 2 tablespoons unsalted butter
- Fresh dill for garnish

For the Tahini Sauce:

- 1/2 cup tahini
- 2 cloves garlic, minced
- 1/4 cup fresh lemon juice
- 1/4 cup water, plus more as needed
- 1 tablespoon olive oil
- Salt and black pepper to taste
- 1 tablespoon chopped fresh parsley (optional)

Instructions:

1. Preheat the oven to 375°F.
2. In a small bowl, mix together tahini, minced garlic, fresh lemon juice, water, olive oil, salt, and black pepper until well combined. Add more water if needed to reach the desired consistency.

3. Season the salmon filets with salt and black pepper on both sides.
4. Heat olive oil in an oven-safe skillet over medium-high heat.
5. Place the salmon filets in the skillet and cook for 4-5 minutes on each side until golden brown and cooked through.
6. Remove the salmon from the skillet and set aside on a plate.
7. In the same skillet, add lemon slices and minced garlic. Cook for 1-2 minutes until fragrant.
8. Add butter to the skillet and stir until melted.
9. Spoon the lemon butter sauce over the salmon filets.
10. Garnish with fresh dill before serving for an extra burst of flavor.
11. Serve the seared salmon hot with your choice of sides or on top of a salad.
12. For added flavor, drizzle tahini sauce over the salmon filets before serving or use it as a dipping sauce on the side.

Broiled Sardines

Ingredients:

- 1 lb fresh sardines, cleaned and gutted
- 2 tbsp olive oil
- 1 lemon, thinly sliced
- 3 cloves garlic, minced
- 1 tsp sea salt
- 1/2 tsp black pepper
- 1 tbsp fresh parsley, chopped
- 1/2 tsp red pepper flakes (optional)

Instructions:

1. Preheat the broiler on high.
2. Pat dry the sardines and place them on a foil-lined baking sheet.
3. In a small bowl, mix together olive oil, minced garlic, sea salt, black pepper, chopped parsley, and red pepper flakes (if using).
4. Brush the mixture evenly over the sardines on both sides.
5. Place lemon slices on top of the sardines.
6. Broil for 6-7 minutes until golden brown and crispy.
7. Serve hot with your choice of sides or as a main dish with crusty bread and a side salad.

Grilled Shrimp

Ingredients:

- 1 lb large shrimp, peeled and deveined
- 3 tbsp olive oil
- 4 cloves garlic, minced
- 1 lemon, juiced and zested
- 1 tsp sea salt
- 1/2 tsp black pepper
- 1 tsp smoked paprika
- 2 tbsp fresh cilantro or parsley, chopped
- 1/2 tsp red pepper flakes (optional)
- Lemon wedges, for serving

Instructions:

1. In a large bowl, mix together olive oil, minced garlic, lemon juice and zest, sea salt, black pepper, smoked paprika, chopped cilantro or parsley, and red pepper flakes (if using).
2. Add the shrimp to the marinade and toss to coat evenly.
3. Cover and let marinate in the refrigerator for at least 30 minutes or up to overnight.

4. Preheat your grill to medium-high heat.
5. Thread the marinated shrimp on skewers.
6. Grill for 2-3 minutes on each side until pink and cooked through.
7. Serve hot with lemon wedges and your choice of sides.

Tilapia Sticks

Ingredients:

- 1 pound fresh tilapia filets
- 1 cup all-purpose flour
- 2 large eggs, beaten
- 1 cup panko breadcrumbs
- 1/2 cup grated Parmesan cheese
- 1 teaspoon garlic powder
- 1 teaspoon onion powder
- 1 teaspoon paprika
- 1/2 teaspoon sea salt
- 1/2 teaspoon black pepper
- Non-stick cooking spray
- Lemon wedges, for serving
- Tartar sauce, for serving

Instructions:

1. Preheat your oven to 400 degrees F.
2. Cut the tilapia filets into strips about 1 inch thick.
3. In a shallow dish, combine panko breadcrumbs, Parmesan cheese, garlic powder, onion powder, paprika, sea salt, and black pepper.
4. In another shallow dish, add beaten eggs.
5. In a third shallow dish, add all-purpose flour.
6. Dredge each fish strip in flour first, then dip in beaten eggs and finally coat with the breadcrumb mixture.

7. Place breaded tilapia sticks on a greased baking sheet.
8. Spray the top of the tilapia sticks with non-stick cooking spray.
9. Bake for 15-20 minutes, flipping halfway through, until golden brown and crispy.
10. Serve hot with lemon wedges and tartar sauce on the side.

Summer-Time Trout

Ingredients:

- 4 fresh trout filets, skin-on
- 2 tablespoons olive oil
- 1 tablespoon fresh lemon juice
- 2 cloves garlic, minced
- 1 teaspoon dried thyme
- 1 teaspoon dried rosemary
- 1 teaspoon sea salt
- 1/2 teaspoon black pepper
- Lemon slices, for garnish
- Fresh herbs (parsley, dill), for garnish

Instructions:

1. Preheat your grill to medium-high heat.
2. In a small bowl, mix together olive oil, lemon juice, minced garlic, thyme, rosemary, sea salt and black pepper.
3. Place trout filets on a large sheet of aluminum foil.
4. Brush the herb mixture onto both sides of the trout filets.
5. Fold up the edges of the foil to create a sealed packet with the fish inside.
6. Place the foil packet on the preheated grill and cook for 10-12 minutes, or until the fish is flaky and opaque.

7. Carefully open the foil packet and transfer the fish to a serving platter.
8. Garnish with lemon slices and fresh herbs.
9. Enjoy your delicious grilled trout in the warm summer weather.

Lemon Trout

Ingredients:

- 4 trout filets
- 1/4 cup olive oil
- 1 tablespoon fresh lemon juice
- 2 cloves garlic, minced
- 1 teaspoon dried thyme
- 1 teaspoon dried rosemary
- 1 teaspoon sea salt
- 1/2 teaspoon black pepper
- Lemon slices, for garnish
- Fresh herbs (parsley, dill), for garnish

Instructions:

1. Preheat your oven to 375°F (190°C).
2. In a small bowl, mix together olive oil, lemon juice, minced garlic, thyme, rosemary, sea salt and black pepper.
3. Place trout filets in a baking dish and brush the herb mixture onto both sides of the fish.
4. Bake for 15-20 minutes, until the fish is flaky and cooked through.
5. Serve with lemon slices and fresh herbs on top.

Enjoy this light and flavorful lemon trout for a refreshing summer meal.

Instant Pot Recipes

Fish Fillet Instant Pot

Ingredients:

- 4 fish filets (such as cod, haddock, or tilapia)
- 1 tablespoon olive oil
- 1 lemon, juiced
- 2 cloves garlic, minced
- 1 teaspoon dried dill
- 1 teaspoon dried parsley
- 1/2 teaspoon paprika
- 1/2 teaspoon sea salt
- 1/4 teaspoon black pepper
- 1 cup vegetable or chicken broth
- Lemon slices, for garnish
- Fresh herbs (parsley, dill), for garnish

Instructions:

1. Turn on the Instant Pot and select the "Saute" function.
2. In a small bowl, mix together olive oil, lemon juice, minced garlic, dried dill, dried parsley, paprika, sea salt, and black pepper.
3. Place fish filets in the Instant Pot and brush both sides with the herb mixture.
4. Pour vegetable or chicken broth into the pot.
5. Close the lid and set the pressure release valve to "Sealing."

6. Select the "Manual" setting and set a timer for 3 minutes on high pressure.
7. Once cooking is complete, use a quick release to release the pressure.
8. Carefully remove the fish from the Instant Pot and place it on a serving dish.
9. Garnish with lemon slices and fresh herbs.
10. Serve hot and enjoy this delicious and quick fish filet made in your Instant Pot.

Brazilian-Style Fish Stew

Ingredients:

- 2 lbs white fish filets (such as cod or tilapia), cut into 2-inch pieces
- 2 tablespoons olive oil
- 1 large yellow onion, finely chopped
- 3 cloves garlic, minced
- 1 red bell pepper, thinly sliced
- 1 yellow bell pepper, thinly sliced
- 2 medium tomatoes, diced
- 1 cup coconut milk
- 1 cup fish or vegetable broth
- 1/4 cup fresh cilantro, chopped
- 2 tablespoons lime juice
- 1 teaspoon smoked paprika
- 1/2 teaspoon ground cumin
- Salt and black pepper, to taste
- Fresh cilantro leaves for garnish
- Lime wedges for serving

Instructions:

1. In a large pot or Dutch oven, heat olive oil over medium heat.
2. Add onions and garlic and cook until softened for about 3-4 minutes.

3. Add red and yellow bell peppers and cook for another 2-3 minutes.
4. Stir in diced tomatoes, smoked paprika, ground cumin, salt, and black pepper.
5. Pour in coconut milk and broth, and stir to combine.
6. Bring the mixture to a simmer and add fish filets to the pot.
7. Cover the pot with a lid and let it simmer for 10-12 minutes or until the fish is fully cooked.
8. Gently stir in lime juice and chopped cilantro.
9. Serve the fish stew hot, garnished with fresh cilantro leaves and a squeeze of lime juice.

Fish Curry (Indian Style)

Ingredients:

- 1 lb (450g) fish filets (such as tilapia, cod, or salmon), cut into bite-sized pieces
- 1 large onion, finely chopped
- 2 tomatoes, chopped
- 1 cup coconut milk
- 2 tablespoons cooking oil
- 1 tablespoon ginger-garlic paste
- 2 green chilies, slit lengthwise
- 1 teaspoon mustard seeds
- 1 teaspoon cumin seeds
- 1 teaspoon turmeric powder
- 1 tablespoon coriander powder
- 1 teaspoon garam masala
- Salt, to taste
- Fresh cilantro, chopped, for garnish
- Fresh curry leaves (optional)
- Lemon wedges, for serving

Instructions:

1. In a large pan, heat oil over medium-high heat.
2. Add mustard seeds and cumin seeds. Once they start to splutter, add in the onions and green chilies.
3. Sauté until the onions turn translucent.

4. Stir in ginger-garlic paste and cook for 1-2 minutes or until fragrant.
5. Add turmeric powder, coriander powder, garam masala, and salt to the pan and mix well.
6. Add chopped tomatoes and cook until they are softened.
7. Pour in coconut milk and bring the mixture to a simmer.
8. Gently add the fish filets to the pan, making sure they are covered in the sauce.
9. Cover the pan with a lid and let it simmer for 10-12 minutes or until the fish is fully cooked.
10. Once done, turn off the heat and stir in some freshly squeezed lemon juice and chopped cilantro.
11. Serve hot with rice or naan bread, garnished with fresh cilantro leaves and curry leaves (if using), and a squeeze of lemon juice on top.

Spinach and Rice Haddock

Ingredients:

- 4 filets of haddock
- 2 cups of spinach, washed and chopped
- 1 cup of basmati rice
- 1 tablespoon of olive oil
- 1 onion, finely chopped
- 2 cloves of garlic, minced
- 1 teaspoon of ground turmeric
- 1 teaspoon of ground cumin
- 1 teaspoon of ground coriander
- 1 teaspoon of smoked paprika
- Salt and pepper to taste
- 2 cups of vegetable or fish broth
- 1 lemon, juiced
- Fresh parsley, chopped (for garnish)

Instructions:

1. Preheat the oven to 375°F (190°C).
2. In a large pan, heat olive oil over medium-high heat.
3. Add chopped onion and minced garlic and cook until softened.
4. Stir in ground turmeric, cumin, coriander, smoked paprika, salt, and pepper.
5. Add chopped spinach to the pan and cook until wilted.

6. In a separate pot, bring vegetable or fish broth to a boil.
7. Stir in basmati rice and reduce heat to low. Let it simmer for about 18 minutes or until all liquid is absorbed.
8. In a baking dish, place the haddock filets and season with salt and pepper.
9. Pour the cooked rice over the fish filets.
10. Top with the spinach mixture and sprinkle some chopped fresh parsley on top.
11. Cover the dish with foil and bake for 20 minutes.
12. After 20 minutes, remove the foil and let it bake for an additional 5-7 minutes or until the fish is fully cooked and flaky.
13. Drizzle freshly squeezed lemon juice over the dish before serving.
14. Garnish with more chopped parsley if desired.
15. Serve hot as a delicious and nutritious meal.

Fish Steak Surprise

Ingredients:

- 4 fish steaks (such as salmon or cod)
- 2 tablespoons olive oil
- 1 large onion, finely chopped
- 3 cloves garlic, minced
- 1 teaspoon turmeric powder
- 1 teaspoon cumin powder
- 1 teaspoon coriander powder
- 1 teaspoon smoked paprika
- Salt and pepper to taste
- 2 cups baby spinach, roughly chopped
- Juice of 1 lemon
- 2 cups cooked basmati rice
- Fresh parsley, chopped (for garnish)

Instructions:

1. Preheat the oven to 375°F (190°C).
2. In a large pan, heat olive oil over medium-high heat.
3. Add chopped onion and minced garlic and cook until softened.
4. Stir in ground turmeric, cumin, coriander, smoked paprika, salt, and pepper.
5. Add chopped spinach to the pan and cook until wilted.
6. In a separate pot, bring vegetable or fish broth to a boil.

7. Stir in basmati rice and reduce heat to low. Let it simmer for about 18 minutes or until all liquid is absorbed.
8. In a baking dish, place the fish steaks and season with salt and pepper.
9. Pour the cooked rice over the fish filets.
10. Top with the spinach mixture and sprinkle some chopped fresh parsley on top.
11. Cover the dish with foil and bake for 20 minutes.
12. After 20 minutes, remove the foil and let it bake for an additional 5-7 minutes or until the fish is fully cooked and flaky.
13. Drizzle freshly squeezed lemon juice over the dish before serving for a zesty flavor.
14. Garnish with more chopped parsley if desired for added freshness.

Tomato Basil and Tilapia

Ingredients:

- 4 tilapia filets
- Salt and pepper, to taste
- 2 tablespoons olive oil
- 1 medium onion, finely chopped
- 3 cloves garlic, minced
- 1 can (14.5 oz) diced tomatoes
- 1 cup fresh basil leaves, chopped
- 1/2 teaspoon dried oregano
- 1/2 teaspoon red pepper flakes (optional)
- 1/4 cup grated Parmesan cheese
- 1 lemon, cut into wedges

Instructions:

1. Preheat the oven to 375°F (190°C).
2. Season tilapia filets with salt and pepper.
3. Heat olive oil in a large pan over medium-high heat.
4. Add chopped onion and minced garlic and cook until softened.
5. Stir in diced tomatoes, fresh basil leaves, dried oregano, and red pepper flakes (if desired).
6. Let the mixture simmer for about 10 minutes or until slightly thickened.
7. In a baking dish, place the seasoned tilapia filets in a single layer.

8. Pour the tomato basil sauce over the fish.
9. Sprinkle-grated Parmesan cheese on top.
10. Cover the dish with foil and bake for 20 minutes.
11. Remove the foil and let it bake for an additional 5-7 minutes until the fish is fully cooked and flaky.
12. Serve with lemon wedges for added flavor.
13. Optional: garnish with additional chopped basil leaves before serving.

Spanish Rice

Ingredients:

- 1 tablespoon olive oil
- 1 small onion, finely chopped
- 1 green bell pepper, chopped
- 2 cloves garlic, minced
- 1 cup long-grain white rice
- 2 cups chicken broth
- 1 can (14.5 ounces) diced tomatoes with green chilies
- 1 teaspoon chili powder
- 1/2 teaspoon cumin
- Salt and pepper to taste
- 1/4 cup fresh cilantro, chopped (optional)
- Lime wedges for serving

Instructions:

1. In a large skillet, heat olive oil over medium-high heat.
2. Add chopped onion and green bell pepper and cook until softened.
3. Stir in minced garlic and cook for an additional minute.
4. Add rice to the skillet and stir until it is lightly coated with oil.
5. Pour in chicken broth, and diced tomatoes with chilies, chili powder, cumin, salt, and pepper. Stir well to combine.

6. Bring the mixture to a boil, then reduce the heat to low and cover the skillet with a lid.
7. Let it simmer for about 20 minutes or until the liquid is absorbed and the rice is fully cooked.
8. If desired, add chopped cilantro to the skillet and stir it in before serving.
9. Serve with lime wedges for added flavor.
10. Optional: You can also add cooked chicken or shrimp to make this dish a complete meal. Simply add them to the skillet when you add the rice and adjust cooking time accordingly.

Instant Pot Broccoli

Ingredients:

- 1 pound fresh broccoli florets
- 1 cup water
- Salt and pepper to taste
- Olive oil or melted butter (optional)
- Lemon wedges for serving (optional)

Instructions:

1. Wash and trim the broccoli florets, if needed.
2. Add one cup of water to the Instant Pot and place a steamer basket inside.
3. Place the trimmed broccoli florets in the steamer basket.
4. Close the lid of the Instant Pot and make sure it is set to sealing mode.
5. Cook on high pressure for 0 minutes (yes, you read that right), followed by quick release.
6. Remove the cooked broccoli from the Instant Pot using tongs or a slotted spoon.
7. Season with salt and pepper to taste.
8. If desired, drizzle some olive oil or melted butter over the broccoli for added flavor.
9. Serve with lemon wedges on the side for a refreshing and tangy twist.

Instant Pot Cauliflower

Ingredients:

- 1 medium head of cauliflower, cut into florets
- 1 cup water
- Salt and pepper to taste
- 1 tablespoon olive oil or melted butter (optional)
- Fresh herbs for garnish (optional)
- Lemon wedges for serving (optional)

Instructions:

1. Wash and cut the cauliflower into florets.
2. Pour one cup of water into the Instant Pot and place a steamer basket inside.
3. Add the cauliflower florets to the steamer basket.
4. Close the lid of the Instant Pot and make sure it is set to sealing mode.
5. Cook on high pressure for 0 minutes, followed by quick release.
6. Once cooked, carefully remove the cauliflower from the Instant Pot using tongs or a slotted spoon.
7. Season with salt and pepper to taste.
8. If desired, drizzle some olive oil or melted butter over the cauliflower for added flavor.
9. Top with fresh herbs for a pop of color and extra flavor.
10. Serve with lemon wedges on the side for a tangy kick.

Split Pea Soup

Ingredients:

- 2 cups split peas, rinsed and sorted
- 1 large onion, diced
- 2 medium carrots, diced
- 2 celery stalks, diced
- 3 cloves garlic, minced
- 1 ham hock (optional for added flavor)
- 1 teaspoon dried thyme
- 1 bay leaf
- 1 teaspoon salt
- 1/2 teaspoon black pepper
- 6 cups chicken or vegetable broth
- 1 tablespoon olive oil
- Fresh parsley, chopped (for garnish)

Instructions:

1. Rinse and sort the split peas, removing any debris or discolored peas.
2. In a large pot or Dutch oven, heat olive oil over medium-high heat.
3. Add diced onion, carrots, celery, and garlic to the pot and sauté until fragrant, about 5 minutes.
4. Add in the rinsed split peas and stir to combine with the vegetables.

5. Pour in broth and add thyme, bay leaf, salt, pepper, and ham hock (if using).
6. Bring soup to a boil then reduce heat to low.
7. Cover and simmer for about 1 hour, stirring occasionally.
8. Once the split peas are soft and the soup has thickened, remove from heat.
9. Discard the bay leaf and ham hock (if used).
10. Use an immersion blender or transfer the soup to a blender to puree until smooth.
11. Serve hot with a sprinkle of fresh parsley for garnish.
12. For added flavor, top with croutons or bacon bits before serving.

Tacos and Lentils

Ingredients:

- 1 cup dried lentils, rinsed
- 1 teaspoon olive oil
- 1 small onion, finely chopped
- 1 bell pepper, diced
- 2 cloves garlic, minced
- 1 teaspoon ground cumin
- 1 teaspoon chili powder
- 1 teaspoon smoked paprika
- 1/2 teaspoon dried oregano
- 1 can (14.5 ounces) diced tomatoes
- 2 cups vegetable broth
- Salt and pepper to taste
- 8 small corn or flour tortillas
- Toppings: shredded lettuce, diced tomatoes, diced avocado, chopped cilantro, crumbled queso fresco, lime wedges

Instructions:

1. In a medium pot, bring 2 cups of water to a boil and add in the rinsed lentils. Reduce heat to low and let simmer for about 15 minutes until tender.
2. While the lentils are cooking, heat olive oil in a large skillet over medium-high heat.

3. Add diced onions and bell pepper to the skillet and sauté for about 5 minutes until softened.
4. Stir in minced garlic, cumin, chili powder, smoked paprika, and oregano, and cook for an additional minute until fragrant.
5. Pour in diced tomatoes (including juices) and vegetable broth into the skillet and bring to a boil.
6. Once boiling, reduce heat to low and let simmer for about 10 minutes until slightly thickened.
7. Add cooked lentils (drained if necessary) to the skillet and stir until well combined.
8. Season with salt and pepper to taste.
9. Warm tortillas in a separate pan or in the microwave until pliable.
10. To serve, spoon the lentil mixture onto each tortilla and top with desired toppings such as shredded lettuce, diced tomatoes, diced avocado, chopped cilantro, crumbled queso fresco, or lime wedges.
11. Fold the tortilla over the filling and enjoy your delicious and nutritious lentil tacos!

Vegetable Soup

Ingredients:

- 2 tablespoons olive oil
- 1 large onion, chopped
- 2 carrots, peeled and chopped
- 2 celery stalks, chopped
- 2 garlic cloves, minced
- 1 zucchini, chopped
- 1 yellow squash, chopped
- 1 red bell pepper, chopped
- 1 green bell pepper, chopped
- 1 can (14.5 ounces) diced tomatoes
- 6 cups vegetable broth
- 1 teaspoon dried thyme
- 1 teaspoon dried basil
- 1 bay leaf
- Salt and pepper, to taste
- 2 cups chopped kale or spinach
- 1 cup frozen peas

Instructions:

1. In a large pot or Dutch oven, heat the olive oil over medium-high heat.
2. Add in the chopped onion, carrots, celery, and garlic and sauté for about 5 minutes until vegetables are softened.

3. Next, add the chopped zucchini, yellow squash, red bell pepper, and green bell pepper to the pot and continue to cook for an additional 5 minutes.
4. Pour in the can of diced tomatoes (including juices) and vegetable broth into the pot.
5. Stir in dried thyme, basil, bay leaf, salt, and pepper to taste.
6. Bring soup to a boil, then reduce heat and let simmer for about 20 minutes.
7. After 20 minutes, stir in chopped kale or spinach and frozen peas into the soup.
8. Let cook for an additional 5-10 minutes until greens are wilted and peas are heated through.
9. Remove bay leaf before serving hot vegetable soup.
10. Serve with crusty bread or crackers for a hearty meal.

Fast Instant Pot Salmon (For Frozen Ones)

Ingredients:

- 4 frozen salmon filets
- 1 cup of water or fish broth
- 1 lemon, thinly sliced
- 2 cloves garlic, minced
- 1 teaspoon dried dill
- Salt and pepper to taste
- 2 tablespoons olive oil
- Optional: Fresh herbs (such as parsley or dill) for garnish

Instructions:

1. Place frozen salmon filets in the Instapot, arranging them so that they do not overlap.
2. Pour 1 cup of water or fish broth into the pot.
3. Season salmon with minced garlic, dried dill, salt, and pepper to taste.
4. Lay lemon slices on top of the salmon filets.
5. Drizzle olive oil over the top of everything in the pot.
6. Close the lid and set the pressure release valve to "sealing".
7. Press the "pressure cook" button and set it for 10 minutes on high pressure for thinner filets or 12 minutes for thicker ones.

8. Once the timer goes off, let the pressure release naturally for 5 minutes before manually releasing any remaining pressure.
9. Carefully remove salmon filets from the Instapot using tongs.
10. Serve hot with a side of your choice, such as rice or roasted vegetables.

Hummus for Instapot

Ingredients:

- 1 cup dried chickpeas
- 4 cups water
- 1/4 cup fresh lemon juice (about 1 large lemon)
- 1/4 cup well-stirred tahini
- 1 small garlic clove, minced
- 2 tablespoons extra-virgin olive oil, plus more for serving
- 1/2 teaspoon ground cumin
- Salt to taste
- 2 to 3 tablespoons water
- Optional garnish: paprika, chopped fresh parsley, and extra-virgin olive oil

Instructions:

1. Rinse and drain dried chickpeas, then add them to the Instapot with 4 cups of water.
2. Close the lid and set the pressure release valve to "sealing".
3. Press the "pressure cook" button and set it for 30 minutes on high pressure.
4. Once the timer goes off, let the pressure release naturally for 10 minutes before manually releasing any remaining pressure.

5. Open the lid and drain the chickpeas using a colander or strainer, reserving some of the cooking liquid.
6. In a food processor or blender, combine cooked chickpeas, lemon juice, tahini, minced garlic, olive oil, cumin, salt, and 2 tablespoons of reserved cooking liquid.
7. Process or blend until smooth and creamy, adding more cooking liquid or water as needed to achieve the desired consistency.
8. Taste and adjust seasoning as desired.
9. Transfer hummus to a serving dish and garnish with a drizzle of extra-virgin olive oil, paprika, and chopped fresh parsley if desired.
10. Serve immediately with pita bread or vegetables for dipping. Enjoy your homemade hummus made in the Instapot!

Salmon and Vegetables

Ingredients:

- 4 salmon filets (about 6 ounces each)
- 1/4 cup olive oil, divided
- 2 tablespoons fresh lemon juice
- 2 teaspoons Dijon mustard
- 2 cloves garlic, minced
- 1 teaspoon dried oregano
- 1 teaspoon dried thyme
- Salt and freshly ground black pepper to taste
- 2 cups cherry tomatoes, halved
- 1 large red bell pepper, sliced
- 1 large yellow bell pepper, sliced
- 1 medium red onion, cut into wedges
- 1 zucchini, sliced
- 1 teaspoon Italian seasoning

Instructions:

1. In a small bowl, whisk together 2 tablespoons of olive oil, lemon juice, Dijon mustard, minced garlic, oregano, thyme, salt, and pepper.
2. Place salmon filets in a zip-top bag and pour marinade over the top. Seal the bag and massage the marinade into the salmon. Refrigerate for at least 30 minutes or up to 1 hour.
3. Preheat the oven to 400 degrees F (200 degrees C).

4. In a large bowl, combine cherry tomatoes, bell peppers, onion wedges, and zucchini slices. Drizzle with remaining olive oil and sprinkle with Italian seasoning. Toss to coat evenly.
5. Spread vegetables evenly onto a greased baking sheet. Bake for 15 minutes.
6. Remove salmon filets from the marinade and discard excess marinade. Place salmon on top of partially cooked vegetables on the baking sheet.
7. Return the baking sheet to the oven and continue cooking for an additional 10-12 minutes, or until salmon is cooked through and flakes easily with a fork.
8. Serve hot, garnished with fresh herbs if desired. You can also pair this dish with a side of rice or quinoa for a complete meal!

Shrimp Paella

Ingredients:

- 1 lb (450g) large shrimp, peeled and deveined
- 2 tablespoons olive oil
- 1 onion, finely chopped
- 1 red bell pepper, diced
- 1 green bell pepper, diced
- 3 garlic cloves, minced
- 2 cups (400g) Arborio rice
- 1 teaspoon smoked paprika
- 1/2 teaspoon saffron threads, soaked in 2 tablespoons warm water
- 1 (14 oz/400g) can diced tomatoes
- 4 cups (1 liter) chicken or seafood broth
- 1 cup (240ml) dry white wine
- 1 cup (150g) frozen peas
- 1/4 cup (30g) chopped fresh parsley
- Salt and freshly ground black pepper, to taste
- Lemon wedges, for serving

Instructions:

1. Heat 2 tablespoons of olive oil in a large, deep skillet over medium heat. Once the oil is hot, add the shrimp in a single layer. Cook for 2-3 minutes on each side until the shrimp turn pink and are fully cooked

through. Remove the shrimp from the skillet and set aside on a plate.
2. In the same skillet, add 1 finely chopped onion, 1 diced red bell pepper, 1 diced green bell pepper, and 3 cloves of minced garlic. Cook for 5-6 minutes, stirring occasionally, until the vegetables are softened and the onions become translucent.
3. Stir in 1 1/2 cups of Arborio rice, 1 teaspoon of smoked paprika, and a pinch of soaked saffron threads. Cook for 1-2 minutes, allowing the rice to get well-coated with the spices and lightly toasted.
4. Pour in 1 can of diced tomatoes (14.5 ounces), 4 cups of chicken or seafood broth, and 1/2 cup of dry white wine. Stir everything together and bring the mixture to a boil. Once boiling, reduce the heat to low and let it simmer for 15-20 minutes, stirring occasionally, until most of the liquid is absorbed and the rice is cooked through to a tender consistency.
5. Stir in 1 cup of frozen peas and the cooked shrimp. Continue cooking for an additional 2-3 minutes, or until the peas are heated through and the shrimp are well incorporated.

6. Season the dish with salt and freshly ground black pepper to taste. Just before serving, sprinkle a handful of freshly chopped parsley over the top for a burst of color and flavor.
7. Serve the dish hot, accompanied by lemon wedges on the side for added flavor. The citrus will brighten the dish and enhance the overall taste. Enjoy your meal!

Tomato Basil Soup

Ingredients:

- 2 tablespoons olive oil
- 1 large onion, chopped
- 3 garlic cloves, minced
- 2 cans (28 ounces each) whole peeled tomatoes
- 2 cups (480ml) vegetable broth
- 1 cup (240ml) heavy cream
- 1/4 cup (30g) chopped fresh basil
- 1 tablespoon sugar
- Salt and freshly ground black pepper, to taste
- Fresh basil leaves, for garnish
- Crusty bread, for serving

Instructions:

1. In a large pot or Dutch oven, heat the olive oil over medium heat. Add the chopped onion and minced garlic and cook for 5-7 minutes, stirring occasionally, until softened.
2. Drain the canned tomatoes and add them to the pot with the cooked onions and garlic. Use a wooden spoon or spatula to roughly break up the whole tomatoes into smaller pieces.
3. Pour in the vegetable broth and bring the mixture to a boil. Reduce the heat to low and let it simmer for 15-20 minutes, allowing all of the flavors to blend.

4. Using an immersion blender or standing blender, puree the soup until smooth. If using a standing blender, you may need to do this in batches.
5. Once the soup is smooth, stir in the heavy cream and chopped basil. Add sugar, salt and pepper to taste.
6. Cook for an additional 5-10 minutes, or until heated through.
7. Serve hot, garnished with fresh basil leaves, and accompanied by crusty bread on the side for dipping. Enjoy your comforting bowl of tomato basil soup!

Kale Soup with Sweet Potatoes and Lentils

Ingredients:

- 2 tablespoons olive oil
- 1 large onion, chopped
- 2 garlic cloves, minced
- 1 large sweet potato, peeled and diced
- 1 cup (200g) dried green or brown lentils, rinsed and drained
- 8 cups (2 liters) vegetable broth
- 1 teaspoon ground cumin
- 1 teaspoon ground coriander
- 1/2 teaspoon smoked paprika
- Salt and freshly ground black pepper, to taste
- 4 cups (about 200g) chopped kale, tough stems removed
- Juice of 1 lemon
- Fresh parsley, chopped, for garnish
- Crusty bread, for serving

Instructions:

1. In a large pot or Dutch oven, heat the olive oil over medium heat. Add the chopped onion and minced garlic and cook for 5-7 minutes, stirring occasionally, until softened.
2. Add in the diced sweet potato and lentils, and stir to coat with the onion and garlic mixture.

3. Pour in the vegetable broth and bring to a boil. Reduce heat to low and let simmer for 20-25 minutes, until lentils are tender.
4. Stir in the ground cumin, coriander, smoked paprika, salt, and pepper to taste. Let simmer for an additional 5 minutes.
5. Add in the chopped kale and lemon juice, and let cook for another 5-10 minutes, until kale is wilted and tender.
6. Serve hot, garnished with fresh parsley, and accompanied by crusty bread on the side. Enjoy your hearty bowl of kale soup with sweet potatoes and lentils!

Instant Pot Lemon Pepper Salmon

Ingredients:

- 4 salmon filets (about 6 ounces each)
- 2 tablespoons olive oil
- 1 lemon, juiced and zested
- 1 teaspoon freshly ground black pepper
- 1/2 teaspoon salt
- 1/2 teaspoon garlic powder
- 1/2 teaspoon onion powder
- 1/4 cup fresh parsley, chopped
- Lemon slices, for garnish
- Fresh parsley sprigs, for garnish

Instructions:

1. In a small bowl, mix the olive oil, lemon juice and zest, black pepper, salt, garlic powder, onion powder, and chopped parsley.
2. Place salmon filets in the Instant Pot and pour the marinade over them. Make sure to coat both sides of the salmon.
3. Close the lid on the Instant Pot and set it to manual high pressure for 8 minutes.
4. Once done cooking, allow for a natural release of pressure for 5 minutes before using quick release to completely depressurize.

5. Serve hot with additional fresh parsley as garnish and lemon slices on top of each filet. This flavorful and easy Instant Pot Lemon Pepper Salmon makes a delicious weeknight dinner option and pairs perfectly with a side of roasted vegetables or rice.

Cheesy Lentils with Brown Rice

Ingredients:

- 1 cup dried brown lentils, rinsed and drained
- 1 cup brown rice, rinsed and drained
- 4 cups vegetable broth or water
- 1 medium onion, finely chopped
- 2 cloves garlic, minced
- 1 cup shredded cheddar cheese (or your preferred cheese)
- 1/2 teaspoon cumin
- 1/2 teaspoon paprika
- Salt and pepper to taste
- 2 tablespoons olive oil
- Fresh cilantro or parsley, chopped for garnish

Instructions:

1. In a large pot, heat olive oil over medium heat. Add chopped onion and garlic and cook until softened.
2. Add brown lentils, brown rice, vegetable broth or water, cumin, paprika, salt, and pepper to the pot. Stir well to combine.
3. Bring mixture to a boil then reduce heat to low and let it simmer for 40 minutes or until the lentils and rice are cooked through.

4. Once cooked, stir in shredded cheese until melted and fully combined with the lentils and rice.
5. Serve hot with fresh cilantro or parsley on top for added flavor and garnish.

Conclusion

Thank you for taking the time to explore our Pescatarian recipes guide. Your dedication to completing this journey is commendable and signifies a genuine interest in embracing a healthier and more sustainable way of eating. By delving into these recipes, you've opened yourself up to a world of culinary delights that not only nourish your body but also respect the environment.

Transitioning to a pescatarian lifestyle is a powerful choice. It's one that seamlessly blends the benefits of a plant-based diet with the nutritional advantages of seafood. This guide has been crafted to help you make this transition effortlessly, offering a variety of recipes that are both delicious and beneficial for your health. From mouth-watering fish tacos to hearty seafood stews, the possibilities are endless and exciting.

Pescatarian cuisine is incredibly diverse and versatile. It allows you to experiment with a wide range of ingredients, flavors, and cooking techniques. This variety keeps your meals interesting and ensures that you're consistently fueling your body with essential nutrients. Seafood, particularly fatty fish like salmon and mackerel, is rich in omega-3 fatty acids, which support heart health, brain function, and overall well-being. Combining these with an abundance of vegetables, whole grains, and legumes, your diet becomes a powerhouse of vitamins, minerals, and fiber.

The beauty of pescetarianism lies in its flexibility. You have the freedom to tailor your meals to suit your preferences and dietary needs. Whether you prefer grilled, baked, steamed, or raw preparations, there's always room for innovation. Don't hesitate to get creative in the kitchen. Experiment with different spices, herbs, and marinades to discover new flavors and textures. The recipes provided here are just starting points; feel free to adjust them according to your taste and seasonal availability of ingredients.

As you continue on this culinary journey, it's important to remember that making gradual changes is key to long-term success. Start by incorporating a few pescatarian meals each week, gradually increasing as you become more comfortable with the new ingredients and cooking methods. Listen to your body and pay attention to how you feel. You'll likely notice positive changes in your energy levels, digestion, and overall health.

Embracing a pescatarian diet also encourages mindfulness about where your food comes from. Choosing seafood from sustainable sources is crucial for the health of our oceans and marine life. Look for certifications like the Marine Stewardship Council (MSC) or Aquaculture Stewardship Council (ASC) when purchasing seafood. Supporting sustainable fishing practices ensures that you are consuming high-quality products while contributing to the preservation of marine ecosystems.

Beyond the physical benefits, a pescatarian lifestyle can be a gateway to cultural exploration. Each seafood dish carries a story, rooted in traditions from around the world. From Mediterranean grilled fish to Japanese sushi, the diversity of recipes allows you to experience global cuisines from the comfort of your kitchen. This culinary adventure not only broadens your palate but also deepens your appreciation for different cultures and their culinary heritage.

Your decision to complete this guide reflects a commitment to making informed and thoughtful choices about what you eat. Continue to seek knowledge and inspiration, try new recipes, and share your experiences with friends and family. Food has an incredible ability to bring people together, and your journey can inspire others to consider healthier and more sustainable eating habits.

We hope this Pescatarian recipes guide has provided you with valuable insights and practical tips that will enhance your dining experience. Remember, this is just the beginning. There are countless more recipes and culinary techniques to explore. Celebrate your progress, enjoy the process, and savor every bite along the way.

Thank you for being a part of this journey. Your enthusiasm and dedication are truly inspiring. Here's to a healthier, happier, and tastier future with pescetarianism at the heart of your culinary adventures. Keep cooking, keep exploring, and keep enjoying the wonderful world of seafood and plant-based dishes.

Frequently Asked Questions for New Pescatarians

What is a pescatarian diet?

A pescatarian diet primarily focuses on plant-based foods, such as fruits, vegetables, nuts, seeds, legumes, and grains, while also including seafood like fish and shellfish. It excludes other forms of animal meat, such as beef, pork, and poultry.

What are the health benefits of a pescatarian diet?

A pescatarian diet offers numerous health benefits, including improved heart health due to the omega-3 fatty acids found in fish, reduced risk of chronic diseases, better digestion from increased fiber intake, and potential weight management benefits. Additionally, this diet provides essential vitamins and minerals, such as vitamin D and B12, often lacking in plant-based diets alone.

How do I ensure my seafood is sustainably sourced?

To ensure your seafood is sustainably sourced, look for certifications from reputable organizations like the Marine

Stewardship Council (MSC) or Aquaculture Stewardship Council (ASC). These labels indicate that the seafood has been caught or farmed using methods that preserve marine ecosystems and support responsible fishing practices.

Can I get enough protein on a pescatarian diet?

Yes, you can easily meet your protein needs on a pescatarian diet. Fish and shellfish are excellent sources of high-quality protein. Additionally, you can incorporate plant-based protein sources like beans, lentils, quinoa, tofu, and nuts into your meals to ensure a well-rounded diet.

What are some quick and easy pescatarian meal ideas?

Some quick and easy pescatarian meal ideas include grilled salmon with a side of roasted vegetables, shrimp stir-fry with brown rice, tuna salad wraps, fish tacos, and seafood pasta. Many pescatarian recipes are simple to prepare and can be made in under 30 minutes, making them perfect for busy weeknights.

Are there any specific nutrients I need to pay attention to on a pescatarian diet?

While a pescatarian diet is generally nutrient-rich, it's important to ensure you're getting enough vitamin B12, iodine, iron, and omega-3 fatty acids. Fish and seafood naturally provide many of these nutrients, but incorporating fortified foods and a variety of plant-based sources can help round out your diet.

How can I make sure my diet remains balanced and varied?

To maintain a balanced and varied pescatarian diet, include a wide range of fruits, vegetables, whole grains, legumes, nuts, seeds, and different types of seafood in your meals. Experiment with various cuisines and cooking techniques to keep your meals interesting and nutritious. Planning your meals and staying mindful of portion sizes can also help you achieve a well-rounded diet.

References and Helpful Links

Rd, K. J. M. (2023, April 24). What is a pescatarian and what do they eat? Healthline. https://www.healthline.com/nutrition/pescatarian-diet

Crichton-Stuart, C. (2023, December 7). What is a pescatarian diet? https://www.medicalnewstoday.com/articles/323907

Rd, E. L. M. (2024b, April 16). 7-Day Pescatarian diet Plan, created by a dietitian. EatingWell. https://www.eatingwell.com/article/7677248/pescatarian-diet-plan/

Dixon, L. (2024, March 29). 39 easy pescatarian recipes. Taste of Home. https://www.tasteofhome.com/collection/easy-pescatarian-recipes/

Loh, A. (2021, May 14). 21 easy pescatarian dinner recipes. EatingWell. https://www.eatingwell.com/gallery/7903109/easy-pescatarian-dinner-recipes/

Cpt, M. F. M. A. (2024, May 30). Should you try the pescatarian diet? Verywell Fit. https://www.verywellfit.com/pescatarian-diet-4174528

Carrick, E. (2021, February 6). Pescatarian tips, advice, and recipes for beginners. BuzzFeed. https://www.buzzfeed.com/eviecarrick/pescatarian-tips-for-beginners

www.ingramcontent.com/pod-product-compliance
Lightning Source LLC
LaVergne TN
LVHW012027060526
838201LV00061B/4499